*T*his book
belongs to

_____

...*a woman who
desires to experience
God's remarkable
power in her life.*

GROWTH AND STUDY GUIDE

The Remarkable Women of the Bible

Elizabeth George

HARVEST HOUSE™ PUBLISHERS

EUGENE, OREGON

Acknowledgments

As always, thank you to my dear husband, Jim George, M.Div.,Th.M., for your able assistance, guidance, suggestions, and loving encouragement on this project.

bout the Author

Elizabeth George is a bestselling author and speaker whose passion is to teach the Bible in a way that changes women's lives. For information about Elizabeth's books or speaking ministry, to sign up for her mailings, or to share how God has used this book in your life, please write to Elizabeth at:

Elizabeth George • P.O. Box 2879 • Belfair, WA 98528
Toll-free fax/phone: 1-800-542-4611
www.elizabethgeorge.com

∽

Contents

A Word of Welcome

~

Please let me welcome you to this fun—and stretching!—
growth and study guide for women like you who want to
nurture a strong faith in God, a faith like that exhibited by
the remarkable women of the Bible. God has preserved their
stories for us—complete with their trials and triumphs—and
He lets you and me in on their powerful messages of hope,
encouragement, and instruction that we can apply to our lives
today.

A Word of Instruction

The exercises in this study guide should be easy to follow
and do. And the best thing is that they center around the
issues and concerns of your daily life. You'll need your copy
of the book *The Remarkable Women of the Bible*, your Bible,
a pen, a dictionary, and a heart ready to listen to and grow
in wisdom. In each lesson you'll be asked to:

- Read the corresponding chapter from your book.

- Answer the questions designed to guide you to a
  better way—God's way!—of handling your life today.

- Create a list of the messages shot straight from God's
  heart to yours through His Word and the life experiences of women like you, married and single, young
  and old.

A Word for Your Group

Of course, you can grow as you work your way alone through the timeless messages presented through the many women of the Bible featured in this book and as you apply them to your life situation today. But I urge you to share the rich and remarkable journey with other women—with your daughters, your friends, your neighbors, your Sunday school class, or women's Bible study. A group, no matter how small or large, offers personal care and interest. There is sharing. There are sisters-in-Christ to pray for you. There is the mutual exchange of experiences. There is accountability. And, yes, there is peer pressure…which always helps us get our lessons done! And there is sweet, sweet encouragement as you share God's remarkable messages with one another and as together you stimulate one another to greater love, wisdom, and good works.

To aid the woman who is guided by God to lead a group, I've included a section in the back of this growth and study guide entitled "Leading a Bible Study Discussion Group."

A Word of Encouragement

The Bible exhorts us to learn from those who have gone before us (1 Corinthians 10:11). And, my friend, the messages from the hearts and lives of the women of the Bible contain timeless wisdom as well as timely advice for you as you walk through life, every phase and stage of it! As you encounter each need and new trial along the way, you'll surprise yourself as you handle it by God's grace and with the wisdom of the ages—wisdom gleaned from your walk alongside the greats, alongside the remarkable women of the Bible.

$\mathcal{F}$airest of All Creation!

> *"Eve...was the mother of all living."*
> GENESIS 3:20
>
> ~

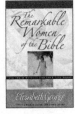 In your copy of *The Remarkable Women of the Bible,* read the chapter that is titled "Fairest of All Creation!" Make notes here about what meant the most to you from this chapter, offered you the greatest challenge, or helped you grow as a woman.

I am created by God for a special purpose + "God don't make no junk."

First Woman

Read the first account of creation found in Genesis 1:1-31 and record what was created each day.

Day 1 (verses 1-5)

Day 2 (verses 6-8)

Day 3 (verses 9-13)

Day 4 (verses 14-19)

Day 5 (verses 20-23)

What was God's observation at the end of Day 5 (verse 21)?

Day 6 (verses 24-31)

What was God's evaluation at the end of Day 6 (verse 31)?

It helps to know that Genesis 1 is a general account of creation. A second account—Genesis 2:1-25—fills in more details, especially those of the sixth day, the day of the woman's remarkable creation. Look at Genesis 2 and write out verse 18.

Now, add additional details for Day 6 found in Genesis 2:18-25.

In your book I asked you to consider what you can do to join with Eve and revel in your lovely womanhood and femaleness. Put your answers here:

Accept your remarkable femininity—

Begin to cultivate your remarkable femininity—

Commit to excelling in your remarkable role as a woman—

First Wife

Eve enjoyed a *joint* role with her husband. What was that role according to Genesis 1:26-28?

And according to Genesis 2:18, what was the first wife's *specific* role?

How does Jesus being the glory of the Father help you relate and accept the fact that a wife is the glory of her husband? (See John 1:14 and 1 Corinthians 11:7.)

First to Fail

Some of the details of "the Fall" are found in Genesis 3:1-6. In a few words, note how the woman contributed to the entrance of sin into the world.

What were the immediate consequences of sin on the woman's life according to verse 16?

Yes, Eve failed! But she went on! How does the knowledge that you have life to give and to pass on to others encourage you to keep on keeping on...even when you fail?

First Mother

Eve acknowledged her dependence on the Lord. How did she express her extreme thankfulness to God for His help (Genesis 4:1)?

Eve also suffered losses during this period in her life. What were they according to...

Genesis 4:1-8—

Genesis 4:13-16—

Regardless of our joys and sorrows, we can—and must!—be thankful to God. State your thankfulness to the Lord as you consider these facts concerning His faithfulness to you:

> ♪ You can trust God in spite of any losses or how you have stumbled and fallen in the *past*.

> ♪ You can trust God with any issue you are facing in the *present*.

❧ You can trust God for whatever happens in the *future*.

First Lessons in Faith

In your book I shared some of my favorite verses about dealing with heartbreaking losses. Using either my verses or your favorites, put their meaning to you in your own words under each of these hope-filled realities:

God's faithfulness (Jeremiah 29:11)—

God's promises (Philippians 4:13)—

God's goodness (Psalm 100:5 or 30:5)—

(P.S. Reread the "resolves and rejoices" and pick out one that particularly applies most to your life today. Write it out here.)

Eve's Message
for Your Life Today

Please read this section in your book again. As you
consider the contents of this chapter and the pressures
or demands of your life, what main message spoke to
your heart...and how can you use that message to better
your life today?

_____

_____

_____

_____

_____

_____

_____

_____

_____

_____

First Steps in Faith

"Abram took Sarai his wife...to the land of Canaan."
GENESIS 12:5

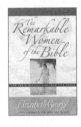
In your copy of *The Remarkable Women of the Bible*, read the chapter that is titled "First Steps in Faith." Make notes here about what meant the most to you from this chapter, offered you the greatest challenge, or helped you grow as a woman.

Whenever you or I get on an airplane to go from point A to point B, we must have faith that the pilots and the plane can get us there safely, don't we? Well, dear friend, as you study your way through these lessons, think of Sarah* as having to trust others with her life, her safety, and her circumstances—a recipe that produced a woman of remarkable faith!

---

* God changes Sarai to Sarah. For consistency, I'll use Sarah throughout
  this study.

Leaving and Cleaving

> Therefore shall a man leave his father and his
> mother, and shall cleave unto his wife: And
> they shall be one flesh (Genesis 2:24 KJV).

Read Genesis 2:24. What do you believe God had in mind
for a marriage according to this verse?

Read Genesis 11:26–12:5. How did Sarah follow this prin-
ciple of "leaving and cleaving"?

Now if you are married, how does your marriage measure
up in the area of "leaving and cleaving"? And what steps can
you take today to trust your husband's leadership in your
life?

Facing Famine

I know I've faced a few famines in my married life. One
particular period was when my husband, Jim, quit his job
to go into the ministry...meaning I went from having much
to having not-much! How about you? I'm sure you've had a
similar time of "famine." How did you manage? What was
your attitude? And what lessons did you learn?

What famine situation are you facing today? How can the **F-A-I-T-H** acrostic (as spelled out below) help?

> **F**ace forward—Are you looking back instead of forward? Please explain.

> **A**ccept your circumstance—Have you accepted your present famine situation as from God? Again, please explain.

> **I**f your circumstances find you in God's will, you will find God in your circumstances—In your present famine situation, do you consider yourself to be in or out of God's will? Is there anything you can do to remedy the situation?

> **T**rust in the Lord——Fear immobilizes, but faith gives confidence. What steps of confident trust can you take today?

> **H**ope for the future—How does the poem "a prayer to pray" give you hope for your future?

Facing Fear

Recall a time when you were afraid for yourself, your children, or your husband. How did you respond to your fear?

Read Genesis 12:10-16. How does God's Word say Sarah dealt with and handled her awkward and potentially disastrous situation? And what does this reveal about her as a wife? About her trust in God?

Trusting in the Lord

Now read Genesis 12:17-20. How did *God* handle Sarah's situation?

How do the following verses help you in the Trust Department?

> Psalm 37:25—

> Proverbs 3:5-6—

> Matthew 19:26—

> 1 Corinthians 10:13—

> 2 Peter 2:9—

Trusting the Lord...Again and Again!

Now scan through Genesis 20:1-17 and compare this situation with that in Genesis 12:10-20. How similar are Sarah's actions in the two accounts?

It's interesting to note that the Bible doesn't comment on the actions of Sarah or Abraham during either of these two similar life situations. We can see the lack of faith in Abraham. But the question is, How do you think you would have responded...if you had been in Sarah's sandals...

...to Abraham?

...to the two kings?

...to God?

Are you facing a difficult issue or situation in your life today? Write it here. Then apply the four lessons of "Pray, Trust, Believe, and Wait" to your problem.

My problem is...

Pray—

Trust—

Believe—

Wait—

Sarah's Message
for Your Life Today

Please read this section in your book again. As you consider the contents of this chapter and the pressures or demands of your life, what main message spoke to your heart...and how can you use that message to better your life today?

_____

_____

_____

_____

_____

_____

_____

_____

_____

_____

Advanced Steps in Faith

"Is anything too hard for the LORD?"
GENESIS 18:14

∾

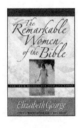
In your copy of *The Remarkable Women of the Bible,* read the chapter that is titled "Advanced Steps in Faith." Make notes here about what meant the most to you from this chapter, offered you the greatest challenge, or helped you grow as a woman.

Reaching for God's Promises

Keep in mind that being childless in our culture is not seen as a big problem—unless you are a woman who wants children! In fact, many women today are purposefully deciding not to have children. But that wasn't the case in Sarah's day. To be "barren" was seen as a curse and a possible judgment of personal sin.

Quickly note God's promises to give descendants to Abraham.

Genesis 12:2—

How old was Abraham when God gave this first
promise to him (see verse 4)?

Genesis 15:4-5—

Genesis 17:6—

How old was Abraham when God repeated His
promise of a child (see Genesis 17:1)?

Genesis 17:15-16—

Genesis 17:19—

Now do the math. According to Genesis 17:17, how many
years will have passed between God's initial promise of
Genesis 12:2 and 4 and its fulfillment?

The remarkable Sarah waited 25 years for something God
promised. Could you? Recap in a few words what you are
learning from Sarah about waiting.

Continuing to Believe

How do these verses about Abraham's faith help you believe God regarding your seemingly impossible situations?

By choice—Romans 4:21

By faith—Romans 4:13

By exercise—Romans 4:20

Look in your Bible at Solomon's benediction on God's people in 1 Kings 8:56. How does it encourage you as you face your problems, your struggles, and your tests of faith today?

Continuing On

As we learned, Sarah's influence is continuing on throughout the generations of all time. How do you respond to the concept of your influence doing the same into the next generations? And what were your thoughts about your own influence as you read about that of Esther Edwards?

What changes do you need to make to ensure that your influence will be more godly?

Answering a Question

Before we ask and answer a question or two, first pause and read Genesis 18:1-2 and 9-14. What was the question the angel asked the doubting Sarah in verse 14?

In the book I asked a number of rhetorical questions that demanded an obvious and resounding *"No!"* for an answer. Now let's turn those questions around and ask them in another way. List your concerns and leave them with God. For instance...

What physical difficulty are you facing that you should entrust to the hands of "the Great Physician"?

What heartache are you suffering that you can place in the lap of the Lord?

What problem in your marriage or family can you give over to God?

What financial problem can the God who owns all "the cattle on a thousand hills" (Psalm 50:10) help solve?

What other problems or issues are you facing this day of your life that you can relinquish to the Lord?

Beloved, remember—no problem is too hard for the Lord!

Sarah's Message
for Your Life Today

Please read this section in your book again. As you consider the contents of this chapter and the pressures or demands of your life, what main message spoke to your heart…and how can you use that message to better your life today?

_____

_____

_____

_____

_____

_____

_____

_____

_____

_____

_____

_____

Rewards of Faith

"And the LORD did for Sarah as He had promised."
GENESIS 21:1 NASB

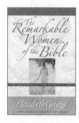
In your copy of *The Remarkable Women of the Bible,* read the chapter that is titled "Rewards of Faith." Make notes here about what meant the most to you from this chapter, offered you the greatest challenge, or helped you grow as a woman.

In this final lesson on the extraordinary life of a truly remarkable woman, we, along with everyone else who cares to read, are witnesses of the rewards of Sarah's faith. Yes, she had her struggles. And she had her low points. But ultimately her faith was rewarded.

Waiting on the Lord

Beloved, as I said in the book, we all are waiting for something. What are *you* waiting for? How does each of these three blessings that follow encourage you in your wait?

Blessing #1: Increased value—

Blessing #2: Increased time—

Blessing #3: Increased faith—

In addition to these three blessings, God has provided other blessings that are also yours as you wait on the Lord. Jot them down now and be even more encouraged in your wait.

Psalm 27:14—

Isaiah 40:31—

Lamentations 3:25-26—

Micah 7:7—

Waiting on the Promises

Read now about the fulfillment of God's promise to Sarah in Genesis 21:1-8. How does it encourage you as you wait on God's promises for you and your life?

And these verses as well?

Hebrews 1:23—

2 Peter 1:3-4—

Waiting on a Miracle

Look now at these promises. How does each encourage you in your trust of the Lord's ability to care for you?

Eternal life: John 10:28—

Sufficient grace: 2 Corinthians 12:9—

Strength for life: Philippians 4:13—

God's everlasting presence: Joshua 1:9—

Waiting on the Reward

We have asked this question in a variety of ways throughout the three lessons highlighting Sarah and her remarkable faith, but it must be asked again. For what, my dear sister, are you waiting? Share it here.

Now how do these verses encourage you to pray while you are waiting?

Matthew 7:7-11—

Luke 18:1—

Hebrews 4:16—

Waiting on Joy

Sarah's long wait ended in unspeakable joy! However, that joy took 25 years to arrive. God promised...and God provided. Truly, Sarah is an awesome example of faith!

Now let's consider your life and all the issues and needs that you face. Think back on a time when God didn't answer your prayers as (or as soon as!) you hoped. Would you characterize your response to God's working as a joyous one? Please explain.

What lessons does Sarah's life have for you?

Remember, too, that joy is a fruit of your spiritual walk with the Lord (see Galatians 5:22). So regardless of your circumstances and your trials, how does James 1:2 say you should respond?

Like Sarah, God has reasons for allowing you to go through difficulties and sorrows. What spiritual blessings have your trials produced in your life? Or, put another way, how has your faith grown through these challenges?

Sarah's Message
for Your Life Today

Please read this section in your book again. As you consider the contents of this chapter and the pressures or demands of your life, what main message spoke to your heart...and how can you use that message to better your life today?

_____

_____

_____

_____

_____

_____

_____

_____

_____

_____

Ready, Willing, and Able!

And Rebekah said, "I will go."
GENESIS 24:58

∾

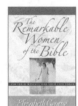 In your copy of *The Remarkable Women of the Bible*, read the chapter that is titled "Ready, Willing, and Able!" Make notes here about what meant the most to you from this chapter, offered you the greatest challenge, or helped you grow as a woman.

Let's look in now on the life of the young single girl, Rebekah, as she embarks on a journey that will take her away from all that is familiar and...into the unknown. She, like Sarah, would be leaving family, friends, and country. But unlike Sarah, who submitted to following her husband, Rebekah is going to *will-fully* take Sarah's same desert journey of some 500 miles. Hang on! Rebekah is another remarkable woman!

Ready to Serve

Let's fast-forward some 40 years after the birth of Sarah's little Isaac. Read Genesis 23:1-2 and describe the scene:

> What request did Abraham make of his oldest and most trusted servant in Genesis 24:1-4?

> Now read Genesis 24:10-59. Where did Eliezer go (verse 10), when did he arrive, and why was it important (verses 11-14)?

Checkpoint on the Journey

Married or single, what is the application of the quote in your book for you?

Willing to Go

Sarah was 90 years old when Isaac was born (Genesis 17:17,21) and 127 when she died (23:1). Now, you do the math.

> How old was Isaac when his mother died?

> And how old was Isaac when he took Rebekah as his wife (Genesis 25:20)?

> What evidence is there that Rebekah went willingly to marry Isaac (Genesis 24:54-58)?

How did Eliezer view God's hand in his match-making endeavors (verse 48)?

Checkpoint on the Journey
Reread this point in your book. What evidence points to your willingness to follow God's will and renounce the world's influence?

Godly in Character
Read Genesis 24:12-14. Eliezer asked God to indicate the woman for Isaac by giving some stipulations. What would these stipulations indicate about the character of the woman?

Checkpoint on the Journey
Reread this point in your book and look up 1 Samuel 16:7 and 1 Peter 3:3-4 in your Bible.

> Why is it more important to focus on godly character than on beauty or affluence?

> What steps can—and will—you take to adjust your standards to match those God sets?

Able to Work

The Bible is filled with admonitions to work, to work hard, to work energetically, to work joyfully, and to work for the Lord. Jot down these exhortations regarding work:

Ecclesiastes 9:10—

Nehemiah 4:6—

Colossians 3:23—

Checkpoint on the Journey

Reread this section in your book. Then read Proverbs 31:10-31.

List several evidences of an ideal work ethic.

How has Rebekah's work ethic and this lesson changed your thinking about your work habits?

Willing to Go the "Extra Mile"

Going the "extra mile" is the attitude of a servant and of Rebekah. What do these verses say about being a servant?

Matthew 5:41-42—

Matthew 20:28—

Galatians 5:13—

Checkpoint on the Journey

Describe a time this week when you went the "extra mile" for someone. If you have yet to go that mile for someone else, ask God to give you the sensitivity to give more than is needed.

Rebekah's Message
for Your Life Today

Please read this section in your book again. As you consider the contents of this chapter and the pressures or demands of your life, what main message spoke to your heart...and how can you use that message to better your life today?

_____

_____

_____

_____

_____

_____

_____

_____

_____

_____

_____

_____

Tests of Faith

> *"And Rebekah said, 'I am weary of my life.'"*
> GENESIS 27:46

~

 In your copy of *The Remarkable Women of the Bible,* read the chapter that is titled "Tests of Faith." Make notes here about what meant the most to you from this chapter, offered you the greatest challenge, or helped you grow as a woman.

Many people have despised going to school for one very traumatic reason—tests! And I relate! I enjoyed most of my schooling...except for my French class. Why? Because every week we had a test. And, more times than not, I would do poorly. Every week that test revealed what I knew and, more importantly, what I *didn't* know! Well, in our current lesson, the remarkable Rebekah is embarking on an amazing journey—a journey with many tests along the way!

Test #1—Leaving All

In a few words of your own, describe the meeting between Rebekah and Isaac (Genesis 24:61-67). Wow!

What positive effect did Rebekah have on Isaac (verse 67)?

Checkpoint on the Journey

How are you doing as a wife in the Positive-Effect-on-Your-Husband Department? Or, in what ways could you improve in the following areas?

Leaving your family and cleaving to your husband—

Helping your husband—

Following your husband—

Respecting your husband—

Test #2—Barrenness

Read Genesis 25:19-21. What 20-year problem cast a shadow on Isaac and Rebekah's bliss?

Everyone (including you and me!) has problems. It's a fact of life. What conclusions can we draw from these few Scriptures when things don't go our way?

Isaiah 55:8-9—

Jeremiah 29:11—

Romans 11:33-34—

Barrenness was a problem with Sarah and also for Rebekah and many other women of the Bible. We will see in the studies to come how these childless women were molded, shaped, and prepared by God and by their test to become His remarkable women of faith and grace.

Checkpoint on the Journey
What problem or issue do you consider to be your test of faith at this time? And how does the fact of God's good plan comfort and encourage you?

Test #3—A Problem Pregnancy
Read Genesis 25:21-24. What was Rebekah's problem, and what was the Lord's explanation for her concerns?

Prayer was a part of Rebekah's life, and there's no doubt prayer should be a vital part of the life of a believer! What do these familiar verses remind us about prayer?

Psalm 4:1—

Matthew 7:7-8—

1 Thessalonians 5:17—

Thought: Asking in prayer helps you look at your problem in the light of God's power, instead of looking at God in the shadow of your problem.

Checkpoint on the Journey

What problem or issue are you taking to the Lord in prayer, and how regularly and resolutely (James 5:16)?

Test #4—Family Problems

After reading Genesis 25:24-28, what is the first clue that there were going to be a few family problems in Rebekah's tent?

What alarming(!) steps did Rebekah go to that further exposed her favoritism (Genesis 27:1-13)?

As you scan through Genesis 27:14-46, what happened to Rebekah's children (verse 41-43) and to Rebekah's heart (verse 46)?

Share five ways a mother or grandmother can guard against favoring one child over another.

—

—

—

—

—

Checkpoint on the Journey

How can you be more faithful to pray for—and appreciate!— each of your children every day?

Test #5—Too Beautiful!

Rebekah was very beautiful. Briefly, according to Genesis 26:1-7, how did her beauty work against her? What happened?

Now read the rest of the story in verses 8-11. How did God come to Rebekah's rescue in this test of faith?

Checkpoint on the Journey

Fear was obviously a problem at this point in Isaac's life! And that fear caused him to fail in the Faith Department and do a terrible thing—lie! How do these Scriptures instruct us to fight our fears with faith in God?

Psalm 56:3—

2 Timothy 1:7—

1 John 4:18—

Rebekah's Message
for Your Life Today

Please read this section in your book again. As you consider the contents of this chapter and the pressures or demands of your life, what main message spoke to your heart...and how can you use that message to better your life today?

_____

_____

_____

_____

_____

_____

_____

_____

_____

_____

Remarkable Mother

The Heart of a Mother

"She hid him three months."
EXODUS 2:2

 In your copy of *The Remarkable Women of the Bible,* read the chapter that is titled "The Heart of a Mother." Make notes here about what meant the most to you from this chapter, offered you the greatest challenge, or helped you grow as a woman.

The Faith of a Mother

Read Exodus 1 and briefly describe the general scene.

Now read Exodus 2:1-9. Notice that no names are mentioned. Who (according to Exodus 6:20) was Amram's wife, and what were the names of their children? (See also Exodus 15:20.)

How did Jochebed show remarkable faith (Exodus 2:1-9)?

What could people point to in your life that would evidence a similar trust in God?

The Courage of a Mother

I have heard it said that *courage is not action in the absence of fear, but action in spite of fear.* This certainly describes the remarkable Jochebed! Look again at Exodus 2:1-9. How did Jochebed show great courage in the midst of a very challenging situation?

How does Jochebed's courage motivate you to take a more active role in the challenges you are presently facing?

The Time of a Mother

We don't know the exact length of time God gave Jochebed with her little Moses. But we do know the outcome of Moses' magnificent life of power and faith as he led God's people to their freedom from bondage: He earned his place in the Bible Hall of Faith (see Hebrews 11:24-25).

If you are a mother, your situation is probably not as dire
or as urgent as that of this mom of a preschooler, Jochebed.
So, let's ask a hard question: How much time are *you* spending with *your* children? With each child or grandchild? (You
may even want to make a time log for a week to get a more
accurate picture of your time with each child.)

What changes do you need to make in your schedule or
lifestyle in order to spend more time with the children God
has entrusted to you?

Remember, the amount of time you spend doing something—
anything!—is an indicator of its value to you.

The Training of a Mother
After reading Deuteronomy 6:5-7, write out God's two basic
guidelines for your life.

Verses 5-6—

Verse 7—

The Work of a Mother
Like Jochebed, you live in an evil and dark world. What
"work" can you do for your family in the following four areas?

Courage—

Creativity—

Care—

Confidence—

The Legacy and the Heart of a Mother

Using these guiding principles from your book, evaluate your adherence to each of the following "commandments."

Commandment #1: Begin early—If your children are older than three, don't be discouraged. Regardless of your children's ages, what one thing can you do today to be the mother God calls you to be?

Commandment #2: Embrace motherhood as an occupation—Even if you have an "outside the home" job, you still must view motherhood as your primary God-given occupation. What will you do today to demonstrate that motherhood is your primary career?

Commandment #3: Live a life of integrity—Your children must see Jesus lived out in you. What steps will you take today to be a more godly model to your children?

Commandment #4: Partner with God—With God's help, you are creating a legacy in your children! How should this affect your daily life and actions? And is there anything you must do or change to leave a stronger legacy of faith?

Jochebed's Message for Your Life Today

Please read this section in your book again. As you consider the contents of this chapter and the pressures or demands of your life, what main message spoke to your heart...and how can you use that message to better your life today?

_____

_____

_____

_____

_____

_____

_____

_____

_____

_____

A Devoted Sister

"And his sister stood afar off,
to know what would be done to him."
EXODUS 2:4

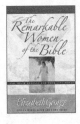
In your copy of *The Remarkable Women of the Bible,* read the chapter that is titled "A Devoted Sister." Make notes here about what meant the most to you from this chapter, offered you the greatest challenge, or helped you grow as a woman.

Tender Loving Care

Read again the account of Moses' birth and rescue in Exodus 2:1-9. As we've learned, Miriam was the sister who stood and watched over her baby brother. Recall and itemize her heroic, energetic, and clever deeds as described in verses 5-9.

Now, in your own words, describe the character qualities you see revealed in Miriam, the devoted sister.

Do you have children? Any 12-year-old types? What steps are or can you take to foster maturity and loyalty in them?

And what can you as a mother do to teach siblings to...

...love one another?

...openly express kindness and concern?

...openly express love?

...cultivate strong family ties?

A Mirror of Her Mother's Merits

Where did Miriam gain her wisdom? We can guess, can't we? From her mother, Jochebed. This spunky, full-of-faith mother defied the pharoah's order to murder her baby. She hid and nourished her baby until she was forced to act quickly and devise a plan and a means for keeping the infant alive.

There's no doubt that a picture is worth a thousand words. As you read the following verses, jot down their central teaching.

1 Corinthians 11:1—

Philippians 4:9—

1 Thessalonians 1:6—

As you soberly evaluate your "merits," list at least two strong qualities you are endeavoring to model (by God's grace!) before your children on a daily basis.

Now note two behaviors you would like to (by God's grace!) eliminate or change.

Devotion to God and to Ministry

As we learned, there is no evidence that Miriam ever married. Instead, we witness in Miriam a life of devotion to God, to family, and to serving God's people...even into her nineties! In your book I asked two questions in this section. Let's answer these questions now.

How effectively am I using my "free" time?

What doors of ministry are open to me now?

Devotion to Family

List several ways you can serve and support your family if you are single. Or if you are a mother, how can you nurture family unity?

A Rare Honor

Besides Miriam, only four others are given the title "prophetess" in the Bible. List them below and add any comments given about them.

>Judges 4:4—

>2 Kings 22:14—

>Luke 2:36—

>Acts 21:9—

Lessons in Leadership

Miriam was a leader among her people. And leadership doesn't just happen. No, there are steps taken all along the way, steps that even you can take! For instance, what can you do to improve in the following ways?

>As a follower—

>As a pray-er—

>As an initiator—

Miriam's Message
for Your Life Today

Please read this section in your book again. As you consider the contents of this chapter and the pressures or demands of your life, what main message spoke to your heart...and how can you use that message to better your life today?

_____

_____

_____

_____

_____

_____

_____

_____

_____

_____

_____

_____

_____

A Devoted Saint

"I sent before you Moses, Aaron, and Miriam."
MICAH 6:4

~

In your copy of *The Remarkable Women of the Bible,* read the chapter that is titled "A Devoted Saint." Make notes here about what meant the most to you from this chapter, offered you the greatest challenge, or helped you grow as a woman.

A Singing Saint

Many of the Bible's heroes of the faith were singing saints. The Israelites sang as they marched, worked, and worshiped. David wrote psalms. Jesus and His disciples sang. The early church had its hymns. And, beloved, you and I will sing forever in the presence of God!

Miriam and her brother Moses sang, too. Read their songs in Exodus 15:1-18 and 15:21. Jot down at least six characteristics of God that Moses and Miriam found worthy of praise.

———   ———

———   ———

———   ———

How can you infuse praise into your daily life? By following the advice of these psalms of praise:

Psalm 34:1—

Psalm 118:24—

Psalm 9:1—

Psalm 69:30—

Now, what verses of praise can you think of that would assist you to praise God more spontaneously and heartily?

Songs in the Night

Look at Psalm 77:6. What was the psalmist's solution for his concerns with his problems during the night?

Read again the quote from Mrs. Elliot on the importance of hymns in times of distress. What can you do this week to make hymns a part of your life and the life of your family?

"God's Songbird"

The next time you are at church, look in the back of the hymnal for a list of songs written by Fanny Crosby. Read through the lyrics of several and notice Fanny's perspective on life...even in the midst of "physical darkness." How does her outlook encourage you in your attitude during the daily trials you face in your life?

A Senior Saint

Miriam served God right into her sunset years. And whenever I think of senior saints like Miriam, I immediately think of "Gramma Kelly." This dear woman spent her time praying for the pastors and the people of my church. When she died at an age nearing 90, the entire church family felt a deep sense of loss not only for her as a person, but also for the loss of a pray-er! Does your church have a senior saint like this? Briefly describe his or her contribution to the life of your church. (Then take a minute to write him or her a personal note of thanks.)

You may not be in the category of "senior saint" quite yet, but, like Miriam (and Gramma Kelly), how are you demonstrating your love for the Lord? For help, consider...

John 14:15—

Psalm 42:1—

What are you doing in the area of involvement or leadership with the women in your church? (Consider Titus 2:3-5.)

The bottom-line question is, Are you heartily serving God's people in your church? (For help, consider Colossians 3:23.)

Epitaph

Quickly read about Miriam's "negative action" in Numbers 12:1-16. What was Miriam and Aaron's accusation against Moses, and why (verses 1-2)?

> Miriam may have led in the rebellion against Moses because she alone was punished by God. What was her punishment (verse 10)?

> What was Moses' response to God's judgment upon Miriam? And what was God's response to Moses' plea (verses 13-15)?

List at least three lessons that leap out to you from Miriam's demise regarding your behavior as a woman in your church. Then thank God profusely for His grace and forgiveness!

Miriam's Message for Your Life Today

Please read this section in your book again. As you consider the contents of this chapter and the pressures or demands of your life, what main message spoke to your heart...and how can you use that message to better your life today?

_____

_____

_____

_____

_____

_____

_____

_____

_____

_____

Remarkable Grace

A Cameo of Courage

Rahab "took the two men and hid them."
JOSHUA 2:4

 In your copy of *The Remarkable Women of the Bible,* read the chapter that is titled "A Cameo of Courage." Make notes here about what meant the most to you from this chapter, offered you the greatest challenge, or helped you grow as a woman.

Before and After

Before—Read Joshua 2:1-21. How is Rahab introduced in verse 1 (and referred to in Joshua 6:17,22,25; Hebrews 11:31; and James 2:25)?

Now briefly describe Rahab's actions in Joshua 2:

    Verses 4-5—

    Verse 6—

    Verses 8-11—

    Verses 12-13—

    Verses 15-16—

    Verse 21—

After—Now read Joshua 6:15-25 and describe Joshua's caution concerning "Rahab the harlot" and her household. Note verse 17 in particular.

    What happened to Rahab and her family after the battle (verse 25)?

    How is God's remarkable grace revealed next (see Matthew 1:5 and 16)?

Your remarkable story—Each of us has a remarkable before-and-after story. Write out these verses from your Bible and then reflect back on *your* life. Pause and pour out your thanks to God for His "remarkable grace."

Ephesians 2:1-2—

Ephesians 1:6-7—

Ephesians 2:8-9—

A Cameo of Courage

Read again Joshua 2:1-7 and list Rahab-the-harlot's acts of faith and courage.

Your remarkable backdrop—What trials and dark events are you experiencing today? How will your faith and courage shine forth as did Rahab's?

A Statement of Faith

Read Rahab's statement of faith in Joshua 2:9-10 and list her beliefs in and about God.

Your statement of faith—Write at least three sentences about what you know God has done for you and for His people.

A Handful of Choices

Your remarkable choices—Read again the poem about "the high way" and consider some of the choices you are making. How does Philippians 1:9-11 encourage and instruct you to make better choices?

Zero in on one of these choices this week! Which one will it be?

The Choice to Help

Rahab's choice to help the spies revealed the following character qualities. As you consider them, list one thing you can choose to do...just for today...in each category. Then, of course, follow through!

Kindness—

Courage—

Faith—

Creativity—

Your choices to help—Read the following verses and comment on what is involved in active faith.

James 1:22—

James 2:14 and 17—

Galatians 6:10—

Is yours an active faith? What choices are you making to help the people of God?

Rahab's Message
for Your Life Today

Please read this section in your book again. As you consider the contents of this chapter and the pressures or demands of your life, what main message spoke to your heart...and how can you use that message to better your life today?

_____

_____

_____

_____

_____

_____

_____

_____

_____

_____

Remarkable Grace

A Portrait of Transformation

"By faith the harlot Rahab did not perish with those who did not believe."

HEBREWS 11:31

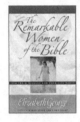

In your copy of *The Remarkable Women of the Bible*, read the chapter that is titled "A Portrait of Transformation." Make notes here about what meant the most to you from this chapter, offered you the greatest challenge, or helped you grow as a woman.

A Chain of Choices

Using a dictionary, look up and write down a definition of "chain."

How do you think faith is like a chain?

Rahab chose to believe the spies—Recall Rahab's remarkable history up to this point, and note three ways she exhibited her budding faith—three "links" in her ever-growing chain of faith.

Joshua 2:4-6—

Joshua 2:8-11—

Joshua 2:12-13—

Your choice to believe—Can you point to any deed performed yesterday that demonstrated your faith in God?

What steps will you take today to "choose to serve the Lord" as Joshua did (Joshua 24:15)? (Name at least two.)

The Choice to Trust

What acts of faith did some people do that merited their presence in Hebrews 11, "Faith Chapter of the Bible"?

Hebrews 11:11—

Hebrews 11:23—

Hebrews 11:31—

Rahab chose to secure a promise. Read Joshua 2:12-14 and note the promise Rahab secured.

Your trust in God's promises—Look in your Bible at the promises mentioned in your book. Then determine if you are acting boldly with a heart of belief.

Hebrews 13:5—

Philippians 4:19—

2 Corinthians 12:9—

The Blessings of Belief

Look again in your book at each of the subheadings below. Then put the brief lists and details into your own words.

Rahab's Life Before Faith—

Rahab's Acts of Faith—

Act of faith #1 (Joshua 2:4)—

Act of faith #2 (Joshua 2:9)—

Act of faith #3 (Joshua 2:12-14)—

Act of faith #4 (Joshua 2:21)—

Rahab's Blessings for Faith

Blessing for faith #1—

Blessing for faith #2—

Blessing for faith #3—

Blessing for faith #4—

Rahab's Life of Faith—

The Transformation Blessing

Since your dictionary is already out, use it again to look up "transformation," and write your findings here.

Rahab's remarkable transformation—What caused Rahab to have each of these labels as a description of her life?

    ❧ A harlot—

❧ A heroine—

❧ A hallowed vessel—

Your remarkable transformation—Dear one, if you believe in the Lord Jesus Christ, you have been redeemed and are being transformed by God's great grace! What do these scriptures tell you about your remarkable transformation?

1 Corinthians 6:11—

2 Corinthians 5:17—

Rahab's Message
for Your Life Today

Please read this section in your book again. As you consider the contents of this chapter and the pressures or demands of your life, what main message spoke to your heart...and how can you use that message to better your life today?

_____

_____

_____

_____

_____

_____

_____

_____

_____

_____

The Path to Greatness

> *"Deborah...was judging Israel."*
> JUDGES 4:4
>
> ∾

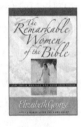 In your copy of *The Remarkable Women of the Bible,* read the chapter that is titled "The Path to Greatness." Make notes here about what meant the most to you from this chapter, offered you the greatest challenge, or helped you grow as a woman.

A Remarkable Woman

Spend the two minutes it takes to read the story of Deborah's life in Judges 4:1–5:31. Check here when done. _____

Now survey Deborah's remarkableness by noting here the contents of these verses.

A remarkable calling—Judges 4:4

A remarkable wife—Judges 4:4

A remarkable wisdom—Judges 4:5

A remarkable leader—Judges 4:14

A remarkable faith—note at least three instances

A remarkable poet—Judges 5:1-3

The path to greatness requires certain qualities. Take the time to consider the "to-do" list drawn from Deborah's life. How are you doing in the following "to be" categories? As you think through each one, write out at least one action you can and will take this week to exhibit these traits of greatness.

Be diligent—

Be devoted—

Be dedicated—

Be available—

Be prepared—

A Remarkable Wife

Write out the central teaching from the following verses that give us God's guidelines for a wife.

Genesis 2:18—

Ephesians 5:22—

Ephesians 5:33—

Titus 2:4—

Are there any areas that you need to work on, any changes you can...or must...make? Write them here.

A Remarkable Witness

Deborah encouraged the Israelites to boldly and obediently follow God. Look at Titus 2:3-5. How does God say you are to spend your time in ministry? And whose faith are you encouraging?

Remarkable Wisdom

According to Proverbs 9:10, what is Step 1 to gaining remarkable wisdom?

And according to Proverbs 2:6, what is Step 2?

According to Proverbs 31:26, what is Step 3?

What, dear one, will you do today to take a giant step toward becoming a woman of great and greater wisdom?

A Remarkable Warrior

Look at the uses of the word *virtuous, excellent,* or *noble* (depending on your translation). These terms which picture a warrior strong in mind and body are also used to describe several remarkable women in the Bible. Also note each scripture's message to your heart.

Ruth 3:11—

Proverbs 12:4—

Proverbs 31:10—

Proverbs 31:29—

A Remarkable Writer

As a benediction to the distinguished life of Deborah, read again through "The Song of Deborah" (Judges 5). What is your favorite line or stanza, and why?

Deborah's Message
for Your Life Today

Please read this section in your book again. As you consider the contents of this chapter and the pressures or demands of your life, what main message spoke to your heart...and how can you use that message to better your life today?

_____

_____

_____

_____

_____

_____

_____

_____

_____

_____

Enduring Difficult Times

"The woman survived her two sons and her husband."
RUTH 1:5

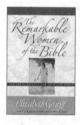 In your copy of *The Remarkable Women of the Bible,* read the chapter that is titled "Enduring Difficult Times." Make notes here about what meant the most to you from this chapter, offered you the greatest challenge, or helped you grow as a woman.

The Seasons of a Woman's Life

Begin acquainting yourself with two more remarkable women by reading Ruth 1:1-5. On the next page, list "the best of times" indicators and "the worst of times" indicators for these dear ladies.

The best of times—

The worst of times—

Naomi...and Ruth, too...tasted the good times and the bad. Everyone does! What encouragement do these verses give you for enduring your own difficult times?

Jeremiah 29:11—

Romans 8:28—

Philippians 3:13-14—

Coping with Tragedy

Read Ruth 1:6-18, noting how God worked in Ruth and Naomi's lives through people, events, and circumstances.

Now make a personal list and relate how God is at work in your life through...

...the people in your life

...the events in your life

...the circumstances in your life

Going Home

Have you heard the saying, "You can become bitter or better"? Look closely at Ruth 1:19-22. What was Naomi's self-description and why?

Relate how the following verses can keep you from being "bitter" and cause you to become "better" as you face your difficult times. (Warning: You may recognize a few of them!)

Jeremiah 29:11—

Ephesians 5:20—

1 Thessalonians 5:17—

2 Corinthians 1:3-4—

"Happenstance"

Moving on through the book of Ruth, read 2:1-11. Who was the person who "happened" into Ruth's life? How did God use this person to better Ruth *and* Naomi's lives?

I made the statement in your book that "there is no such thing in the life of God's children as happenstance or coincidence. There is only the great sovereignty of God Almighty, who watches over His children and guides their steps, sometimes quite obviously...and other times not so obviously." Now, write out the *Look...Believe...and Trust* formula.

Look...

Believe...

Trust...

Once again, be sure to put these truths to work in your present problems!

Under His Wings

You'll love Ruth 2:12-23! Read it now. Then note how God is portrayed in Psalm 36:7.

List the ways God used Boaz to care for Ruth.

God cares for you in the same way. Again, pinpoint any present difficulties. What principles covered thus far can help you to better cope with that situation?

As we pause now in our "gleaning" from the the humble, difficult lives of dear Ruth and Naomi, read "Ruth's Hymn" (Ruth 1:16-17) and "Boaz's Hymn" (Ruth 2:12). How is your trust, dependence, and reliance on God stimulated by theirs?

Ruth and Naomi's
Message for Your Life Today

Please read this section in your book again. As you consider the contents of this chapter and the pressures or demands of your life, what main message spoke to your heart...and how can you use that message to better your life today?

_____

_____

_____

_____

_____

_____

_____

_____

_____

_____

Chapter 14

Enjoying God's Blessings

> *"Blessed be he of the LORD,*
> *who has not forsaken His kindness*
> *to the living and the dead!"*
> RUTH 2:20

In your copy of *The Remarkable Women of the Bible,* read the chapter that is titled "Enjoying God's Blessings." Take notes here about what meant the most to you from this chapter, offered you the greatest challenge, or helped you grow as a woman.

The Kindness of the Lord

Kindness is an attribute of God, and we see this God-like quality demonstrated by Boaz in Ruth 2. What does Boaz say about Ruth and her kindness in Ruth 3:10?

What is said of the woman in Proverbs 31:26?

And in the New Testament, what are we as believers to do according to Colossians 3:12?

Love for One Another

Read Ruth 3:1-5 and 16-18. Ruth and Naomi were truly portraits of selflessness toward each other. Note as you read how they wanted the best for one another.

Now put down the names of several others you can start demonstrating acts of service for today.

A Virtuous Woman

The list of virtues shared by Ruth and the Proverbs 31 woman is quite a list! Look at it again (pages 155-56 in your book) and write down several areas where you need improvement. Then note what you will do about each.

A Virtuous Man

Whether you are married or not, please read Ruth 4:1-13 and review the character qualities of the "virtuous man" listed in your book. What three do you consider to be most important and why?

What should these qualities mean to...

>...a married woman concerning prayer for her husband?

>...a mother concerning her sons?

>...a single woman concerning the men she spends time with?

A Grandmother's Heart

Oh, how I (a grandmother of five toddlers!) love Ruth 4:14-16! How wonderful for Ruth to welcome and involve Naomi in the care of her precious babe! And how equally wonderful for Naomi to help out and to share in nurturing that little one! There is a message here for every mother *and* grandmother! Copy out the acrostic **G-R-A-N-D** below.

G

R

A

N

D

If you are privileged to be a grandmother, how are you living out the "grand" in grandmothering? Be honest, and note any changes that must be made. And if you are a mother, how are you allowing and involving your parents and in-laws in your children's lives?

Bonus question: If you have a grandmother or two in your life, what can and will you do to show your appreciation to them?

Stars in Her Crown

As we end Ruth, a jewel of a book of the Bible, read 4:17-22. In what ways are you encouraging, nurturing, and supporting the "stars in your crown" through...

...fervent prayer?

...mighty encouragement?

...abundant information about Jesus Christ?

...hearty support in their spiritual growth?

Ruth and Naomi's Message
for Your Life Today

Please read this section in your book again. As you consider the contents of this chapter and the pressures or demands of your life, what main message spoke to your heart...and how can you use that message to better your life today?

_____

_____

_____

_____

_____

_____

_____

_____

_____

A Weaving of Grace

"Hannah...prayed to the LORD."
1 SAMUEL 1:10

~

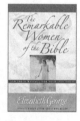

In your copy of *The Remarkable Women of the Bible,* read the chapter that is titled "A Weaving of Grace." Make notes here about what meant the most to you from this chapter, offered you the greatest challenge, or helped you grow as a woman.

Threads of Pain

As we step into the life of another truly remarkable woman of God, the first words about this dear lady are dark, painful ones. What do you learn about her in 1 Samuel 1:1-6?

Name—

Marital and family status—

Daily difficulties—

Now read again the poem "The Divine Weaver" and jot down a few details of your life and daily difficulties. How is God at work weaving the threads of your life together?

Threads of Reverence

Hannah had a problem. No, Hannah had a whole list of problems! Read about them in 1 Samuel 1:7-9. How did she handle her difficulties? What did she do about her "threads of pain"?

A Rope of Prayer

Once she arrived at "the tabernacle of the LORD" (verse 9), Hannah went into action. She had some serious business to take care of with God. Read 1 Samuel 1:10-18. Describe the following:

Hannah's condition (verse 10)—

Hannah's solution (verse 10)—

Hannah's vow (verse 11)—

Hannah's method of prayer (verse 13)—

Hannah being misunderstood (verse 14)—

Hannah's explanation (verses 15-16)—

Hannah's blessing (verse 17)—

Hannah's change of heart (verse 18)—

Dear one, Hannah took hold of the rope of prayer in her hour of greatest need. What is your need today? Write it down and take it to the Lord in prayer!

Threads of Devotion

Backtrack and look long and hard at Hannah's vow in 1 Samuel 1:11. How specific was her prayer request?

This is a classic "if–then" request and commitment. *If* God chose to graciously grant Hannah her request, *then* what would she do?

Note the final words of Hannah's vow. What did she say would be unique about the baby boy?

Just a note: This statement refers to a "Nazarite vow," a vow taken by someone who was separated unto the Lord for special service (see Numbers 6:1-5).

Hannah sets a strong example of devotion to God for all women for all times! Check your heart, my friend. And check your prayers (see James 4:2-3)! For what are you asking… and why? Could you give up the greatest joy and desire of your heart? Could you hand it over to the Lord? Pray to walk in Hannah's footsteps of faith and devotion.

Threads of Faith

Dear Hannah evidenced her faith in 1 Samuel 1:17-18.

How?

What had changed?

What do you think made the difference?

What humanly unhappy "things" are happening in your life today? And how does Romans 8:28-29 encourage your faith?

How are the threads of your faith? What situations do you need to trust God for today? Record three promises given to you in God's Word that can, will, and do strengthen the oh-so-needed threads of remarkable faith.

—

—

—

Hannah's Message
for Your Life Today

Please read this section in your book again. As you
consider the contents of this chapter and the pressures
or demands of your life, what main message spoke to
your heart…and how can you use that message to better
your life today?

_____

_____

_____

_____

_____

_____

_____

_____

_____

Threads of Sacrifice

"I also have lent him to the LORD;
as long as he lives he shall be lent to the LORD."
1 SAMUEL 1:28

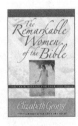 In your copy of *The Remarkable Women of the Bible,* read the chapter that is titled "Threads of Sacrifice." Make notes here about what meant the most to you from this chapter, offered you the greatest challenge, or helped you grow as a woman.

Threads of Joy

In our last lesson we left dear Hannah in Shiloh, praying in the tabernacle of the Lord. What was the prayer of Hannah's heart? What was her response upon receiving a blessing from Eli, the priest (1 Samuel 1:11 and 17-18)?

Continue on now through the life of Hannah by reading
1 Samuel 1:19-20.

> How did God honor her request?

> And how did Hannah choose to remember God's
> gracious answer to her heart-request (verse 20)?

> What does James 1:2 say your attitude should be
> when you encounter trials and tribulations?

> As a Christian, who is your attitude's source accord-
> ing to Galatians 5:22?

Threads of Love

As you read through 1 Samuel 1:21-23, record how Hannah
demonstrated her love for little Samuel.

Using the "guidelines for child-raising" as a checklist, look
up the scriptures noted. If you have children, how are you
doing in the Child-Training Department?

> Loving God with all your heart (Deuteronomy 6:5)?

> Teaching your child God's Word (Deuteronomy 6:7)?

> Teaching your child God's ways (Proverbs 22:6)?

Remembering the Lord at all times (Deuteronomy 6:7)?

Worshiping the Lord—How important was this to Hannah's family in 1 Samuel 1:7,19,21 and 2:19?

Star the one that needs your most urgent attention!

Threads of Sacrifice

Now look at 1 Samuel 1:24-28 and record Hannah's explanation for bringing her son to Shiloh.

Hannah gave the sacrifice of her son. Now how about you? What further sacrifice(s) might God be asking of you regarding...

...your children?

...your obedience?

...your time?

...your money?

Threads of Glory

We see Hannah's perspective on "lending" her son to the Lord. Hannah herself said, "My heart rejoices in the LORD." What glory God receives when we "rejoice in the Lord," even in the midst of sacrifice! Now read—and revel in—Hannah's song of thanksgiving (1 Samuel 2:1-10). Then read Mary's song in Luke 1:46-56. Note the similarities below:

Hannah's Song	**Mary's Song**

What can you learn from these two remarkable women and their two remarkable songs about rejoicing in praise and thanksgiving for the "great things" God has done?

Threads of Vision

Take a minute to jot down the actions Hannah took to show her love to her son Samuel (1 Samuel 2:19).

What, dear mother, can you do to show your love to your children whether they live under your roof, down the street, or across the country?

Threads of Growth

Oh, joy! How did God repay Hannah's obedience to her vow (1 Samuel 2:21)? How does this act of faithfulness on God's part strengthen your faith?

Hannah's Message
for Your Life Today

Please read this section in your book again. As you consider the contents of this chapter and the pressures or demands of your life, what main message spoke to your heart...and how can you use that message to better your life today?

_____

_____

_____

_____

_____

_____

_____

_____

_____

_____

_____

Remarkable Courage

The Beauty of Courage

"If I perish, I perish!"
ESTHER 4:16

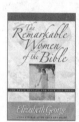 In your copy of *The Remarkable Women of the Bible,* read the chapter that is titled "The Beauty of Courage." Make notes here about what meant the most to you from this chapter, offered you the greatest challenge, or helped you grow as a woman.

The Beauty of Usefulness

Quickly scan Esther 1:1–2:4 and tell how Esther came to be in the palace of the king.

As you read Esther 2:5-20, note several sterling qualities that begin to emerge in Esther's life.

Having considered the details of Esther's life, evaluate the details of your life. How has God worked in your life through...

...your heritage?

...your parentage?

...your tutelage?

...your advantage?

And what are you doing to pay homage to God for these remarkable details of your life?

The Beauty of Courage

God's chosen people, the Jews, were in danger. Who was responsible for their danger, and what did he request of the king (Esther 3:8-9)?

In light of the danger, what was Mordecai's request in Esther 4:7-9?

How was Esther's courage tested in verses 10-11?

And what were Mordecai's wise words of exhortation to Esther in verses 13-14?

Finally, what famous and courageous statement did Esther make in verse 16?

In what ways does Esther's courage strengthen your own courage to live the Christian life? Note at least three.

—

—

—

The Beauty of Wisdom

Courage is best tempered by wisdom. This is definitely seen as Esther steps out with courage marked by the beauty of wisdom. Courage...and wisdom...is always a necessary part of life, but wisdom keeps courage from becoming foolhardy. Observe now how Esther's courage was demonstrated in two wise decisions.

Decision #1—Esther 5:1-8. What was Esther's first request of her husband, the king?

Decision #2—Esther 7:1-6. What was Esther's second request of her husband, the king?

Bonus assignment: Write out what I call "The Seven Steps of Wisdom" on a 3" x 5" card. Refer to them, read them, and pray through them the next time you need wisdom and courage in dealing with stressful people, events, or circumstances.

The Beauty of God's Plan

The evil Haman was dead...but his evil plan was still in force! Now, are you wondering how God used His faithful servants Esther and Mordecai to complete a bigger picture and turn tragedy into triumph? For answers, read Esther, chapter 8, and note...

...the king's gesture (verses 1-4)

...Esther's request (verses 5-6)

...the king's response (verses 7-10)

And now for you! Would you consider yourself to be "faithful where you are, doing your duty"? Does anything need improvement? Note it here.

Do you see yourself as a part of God's bigger picture? How do Ephesians 2:10 and 2 Timothy 2:8-9 help you in your "vision" for your usefulness to God and His people?

The Beauty of Remembering

What was the outcome of the Jewish defense of their lives and possessions according to Esther 9:2-5?

And what did Mordecai do in Esther 9:20-22 to commemorate the victory over their enemies?

The Jews, to this day, remember the events that occurred during the time of Esther. What can you do today to remember God's involvement in your life and the life of your family? (And as a grand finale to this lesson, take a few lines here and now to remember the circumstances surrounding the grand event of your salvation through Jesus Christ!)

Esther's Message
for Your Life Today

Please read this section in your book again. As you
consider the contents of this chapter and the pressures
or demands of your life, what main message spoke to
your heart...and how can you use that message to better
your life today?

_____

_____

_____

_____

_____

_____

_____

_____

_____

_____

Remarkable Walk

Consecrated to God

Elizabeth was "righteous before God, walking in all the commandments and ordinances of the Lord blameless."
LUKE 1:6

~

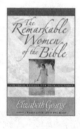

In your copy of *The Remarkable Women of the Bible,* read the chapter that is titled "Consecrated to God." Make notes here about what meant the most to you from this chapter, offered you the greatest challenge, or helped you grow as a woman.

To the Glory of God

My guess is that it will take you all of two minutes to read Luke, chapter 1. So dive in, do it...and delight in it! Check here when done. _____

Now for dear Elizabeth! Write out Luke 1:6, God's description of this remarkable woman. Truly her life gave glory to God!

As you consider verse 7, what makes this description even more remarkable?

More Than a Conqueror

Now back up to verse 6. Using your dictionary, write out a definition of the words...

...righteous—

...blameless—

...obedient—

What does Galatians 5:16 and 22-23 say about our conduct if we are "walking by the Spirit"?

Just a note: As a believer in Jesus Christ, you have a righteous standing with God because of your relationship with Jesus. However, that relationship and positional standing does not negate your responsibility to obey God's commands to "walk by the Spirit" and to "grow in the grace and knowledge of our Lord and Savior Jesus Christ" (see Galatians 5:16 and 2 Peter

3:18). Exactly how are you following through on these responsibilities today?

Strength for Today

Can you imagine (or perhaps relate to!) what each new day, month, year (indeed, a life!) of barrenness must have meant to dear Elizabeth? How she must have felt? But, glory to God(!), He helps us find strength for each day and its difficulties. What do you learn from...

...Nehemiah 8:10?

...Psalm 30:5?

...Lamentations 3:22-23?

Now, dear one, are you utilizing these promises from God to your heart in your situation?

Bright Hope for Tomorrow

More glory to God! He who has been silent for 400 years broke His silence...and miraculously communicated to—of all people!—the lowly Elizabeth and her husband! Marvel as you walk with these consecrated saints through Luke 1:8-25.

When did God communicate to Zacharias (verses 8-9)?

What was occurring at that "hour" (verse 10)?

Who appeared to bring the message of hope (verse 11)?

How did Zacharias respond (verse 12)?

What was the good news (verse 13)?

What were a few of the details regarding the child (verses 13-17)?

What was the mission of their son to be (verse 17)?

What did Zacharias say...and what was the angel's response (verses 18-20)?

What happened next (verse 22)?

How did this scene end...or...was it the beginning (verses 23-25)?

How did the angel's message signal not only bright hope for Elizabeth and Zacharias' lives, but for all mankind, including you?

Remarkable Walk of Faith

Elizabeth's entire life was one remarkable walk of faith. Let's revisit the scriptures and the many stepping-stones Elizabeth's great faith required. Ask God to burn her actions of faith into your heart!

Elizabeth continued on in a righteous, obedient, and blameless walk with God...even when her heart was hurting due to being barren through her child-bearing years. What causes your heart to hurt, precious sister, and how does Elizabeth's example encourage you?

Elizabeth believed God...even when her husband didn't! Has this ever happened to you? What did you do, and what advice does 1 Peter 3:1 give concerning your speech?

Elizabeth hid in quiet joyous seclusion and devotion while waiting on God and on her remarkable, miraculous baby! How do you tend to handle good news—in humble gratitude...or boisterous bragging? Which is the better way?

Elizabeth spoke up and named her little one "John" in obedience to the angel's instructions (and against the peer pressure of friends, family, and well-wishers!). There is "a time to keep silence, and a time to speak" (see Ecclesiastes 3:7). In which direction do you need God's help and wisdom?

Elizabeth's Message
for Your Life Today

Please read this section in your book again. As you consider the contents of this chapter and the pressures or demands of your life, what main message spoke to your heart...and how can you use that message to better your life today?

_____

_____

_____

_____

_____

_____

_____

_____

_____

_____

Highly Favored One

"You have found favor with God."
LUKE 1:30

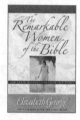
In your copy of *The Remarkable Women of the Bible,* read the chapter that is titled "Highly Favored One." Make notes here about what meant the most to you from this chapter, offered you the greatest challenge, or helped you grow as a woman.

Blessed Among Women

Why is Mary so remarkable? To catch a remarkable glimpse, read Matthew 1:1-16. What does verse 1 reveal this list to be?

And how does this list end in verse 16?

Now, in your own words, why is Mary so remarkable?

Our next obvious question is, Why did God choose Mary for such a remarkable mission? Or, put another way, what kind of woman was Mary? Find out by reading Luke 1:26-38 and then writing out what the Bible says in...

...verse 26—

...verses 27,34—

...verses 28,30—

...verse 38—

What is God's focus according to 1 Samuel 16:7, and how does this encourage you?

Priceless Passion

Yes, Mary was young and probably poor. But she possessed a priceless passion for God. How did Mary's passion display itself in Luke 1:46-55, in her "song," in her "Magnificat"? And while you are enjoying this "praise and worship" song, jot down how and why Mary praised and worshiped God.

Extraordinary Love

There are many reasons God picked Mary to carry and mother His Son, but one of them was Mary's extraordinary love for God. And because of that love, how did the angel address Mary in Luke 1...

...verse 28 (look for two answers here)?

...verse 30?

How did Mary's Son, Jesus, define love in John 14:15?

Here's an item for prayer: "Lord, is my love for You an extraordinary love? Is mine an obedient heart?"

Turning Points

Look now at Luke 1:28. What are the few opening words used to describe the remarkable day that became a turning point for Mary...and for all mankind?

The drama increases! *Who* delivered God's message to Mary (verse 26)?

Again, according to verses 31-33, *what* was about to occur?

And *how* would it take place (verse 35)?

The Heart of a Handmaiden

Hmmm. Do you ever wonder what was racing through Mary's mind at this point? True, she had one question, a perfectly natural and logical one. What was it (verse 34)?

But more important than what was racing through Mary's mind was what was at the core of Mary's *heart!* In the end, how did she answer the angel Gabriel...and God (verse 38)? Write her famous words of complete commitment to the will of God here.

Read again the definition of a maidservant in your book. What strikes you most?

Now look at Psalm 123:2 at a reference to a hand-maiden and her relationship with her mistress. What did the handmaiden do?

How do you see Mary as "the maidservant of the Lord," and how do her words demonstrate the heart of a handmaiden?

Here's another item for prayer: "Lord, work in my heart! Create in me the heart of a handmaiden! Enable me to wholeheartedly embrace Your plan for my life...no matter what!"

An Attitude of Acceptance

Again, what words did Mary declare to Gabriel that indicated an attitude of acceptance (Luke 1:38)?

Answer now the questions at the end of your lesson—answers that will indicate your attitude...or lack thereof...of acceptance to God's will for your life.

      🌿 How do you generally handle shocking news or unfair circumstances?

      🌿 What keeps you from replying to the events of life with "let it be to me according to your word"?

      🌿 What could you do to learn more about the character of our trustworthy God?

      🌿 What step toward that goal will you take today?

Mary's Message
for Your Life Today

Please read this section in your book again. As you consider the contents of this chapter and the pressures or demands of your life, what main message spoke to your heart...and how can you use that message to better your life today?

_____

_____

_____

_____

_____

_____

_____

_____

_____

_____

_____

_____

O Worship the King!

"My soul magnifies the Lord."
LUKE 1:46

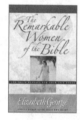 In your copy of *The Remarkable Women of the Bible,* read the chapter that is titled "O Worship the King!" Make notes here about what meant the most to you from this chapter, offered you the greatest challenge, or helped you grow as a woman.

May and December

As a jumping-off point for this magnificent lesson from the life of Mary, the mother of our Lord Jesus, read Titus 2:3-5. What role does God give to "the older women" in the church?

Read now Luke 1:39-45. And just as a refresher, jot down Elizabeth's age (Luke 1:7 and 36).

Also note Elizabeth's miraculous condition as reported by the angel Gabriel to Mary about her cousin in verse 36.

As Mary crossed the threshold to Elizabeth's home, what happened first (verse 41)?

How did the older Elizabeth encourage the young Mary (verses 42-45)?

The Sanctity of Solitude

Elizabeth's pregnancy was a miracle! And yet she chose not to shout her good news from the housetops. What did she do instead, according to Luke 1:24-25?

Months later, when the miraculously pregnant Mary entered Elizabeth's house, what happened (again, see verses 42-45)? Do you think such an outburst and outpouring of Spirit-filled, divine information just might have come as a result of Elizabeth nurturing her soul in private worship? We don't actually know, yet I wonder...

Souls Drawn Upward

What does Luke 1:41 say was the source of Elizabeth's greeting, words, and blessing upon Mary?

And how did Mary's mouth reveal the same source as prose flooded from her heart and lips (verses 46-55)?

What an encouraging time this must have been for both women! How long did their visit last according to verse 56?

Now, the next time you are with another Christian woman, how could and should you use your time? List at least three activities. And remember, everyone needs encouragement!

—

—

—

Heart Song

Look in your Bible at Luke 6:45. As you prayerfully and carefully read through Mary's heart song—her "Magnificat" (Luke 1:46-55)—what do you witness pouring forth from the treasure of her heart?

What instruction do you receive regarding your own heart...and mouth?

Hallelujah, What a Savior!

Write out Luke 1:45 here.

What shocking words! Please add your personal remarks concerning the truths from the verses used to spell out the message of God our **S-A-V-I-O-R**.

S—2 Corinthians 5:21

A—John 10:28-29

V—2 Timothy 2:26

I—Galatians 4:4-6

O—Romans 6:1-10

R—2 Corinthians 5:19

As I asked in your book, Are you saved? Do you enjoy in Jesus Christ all that the word *Savior* represents? Beloved, this is the most important question in this entire *Growth and Study Guide,* indeed, in the universe! And your response is the most important answer you will ever give in your life. What is your answer? Can you exult along with Mary, "Hallelujah, what a Savior!"?

The Beauty of Worship

I have to admit a "pet peeve" to you, my reading friend! It bothers me when I hear someone pray with words like these:

"O God, we want to thank You for who You are and for what You have done!" I always wonder...well, why don't you go ahead and say something about *who* He is and *what* He has done? Why not go ahead and worship Him? Mary had no problem thinking up 10-plus verses of pure worship—specific worship!—along with 15 Scripture quotations from the Old Testament! O, the beauty of worship!

But there are other ways to "worship the King," simple acts that can be offered up to God—as simple as a cup of water given in His name (Mark 9:41) or any deed done heartily as to the Lord and not to men (Colossians 3:23). For instance, what can you give to God as an act of worship in terms of...

...your time?

...your money?

...your faith?

...your witnessing?

...your praise?

O worship the King now...in as many ways as you can!

Mary's Message
for Your Life Today

Please read this section in your book again. As you consider the contents of this chapter and the pressures or demands of your life, what main message spoke to your heart...and how can you use that message to better your life today?

_____

_____

_____

_____

_____

_____

_____

_____

_____

_____

A Woman After God's Own Heart

"And she brought forth her firstborn Son."
LUKE 2:7

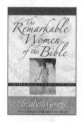 In your copy of *The Remarkable Women of the Bible,* read the chapter that is titled "A Woman After God's Own Heart." Make notes here about what meant the most to you from this chapter, offered you the greatest challenge, or helped you grow as a woman.

The Path of Faith

As we step into yet another look at the life and heart of Mary, see Acts 13:22. How did God refer to David, and how did He define such a one?

Now prepare yourself to meet in Mary, *a woman after God's own heart!*

True Treasure

Begin now by reading Luke 2:1-7, commonly referred to as "The Christmas Story." In your own words, what difficulties did Mary encounter during her birth experience?

And how did God work everything out regarding...

...Joseph?

...the timing of the tax?

...the place of birth (see Micah 5:2)?

...the birth itself?

Now, what is *your* present seemingly impossible situation?

How does Mary's story encourage your heart?

And how do you see God at work in caring for you?

Remember Gabriel's words to Mary in Luke 1:37! Write them here...and on the tablet of your heart!

True Treasure

What group of people were the first to know of Messiah's birth? To find the startling answer, read Luke 2:8-20 and record your answer here.

What miraculous announcement did they hear? (Luke 2:9-14)?

And how did the shepherds respond to "the Good News of Jesus Christ" (verses 15-18)?

And how did others respond (verse 18)?

How did Mary respond (verse 19)?

Now, how much of God's Word are you treasuring up in your heart...to be pondered over in the days and hard times ahead? And how can and will you increase the amount of your treasure?

A Woman After God's Heart

Again, write out what a man (or woman!) after God's own heart is according to Acts 13:22. As you read Luke 2:21-24, list the many ways you witness Mary and Joseph fulfilling God's revealed will as recorded in His Word in the Old Testament law...and communicated to them through the angel Gabriel.

Beloved, if there is *any* area in your life where you are knowingly violating or failing to follow God's clear, revealed instruction for your life, please stop it, put it away, turn from it, and be a woman who follows after God's own heart!

Check your commitment in the following areas and then make your plans to improve:

to your husband—

to your children—

to your church—

to your work—

to your spiritual growth—

The Price of God's Favor

Look now at Mary's encounter with Simeon in Luke 2:25-35.

First of all, what kind of man was he (verse 25)?

And where did they meet (verse 27)?

Why was he so joyful (verses 28-32)?

And what note of sorrow did he share with Mary (verse 35)?

Suffering is a fact of life! Mary's Jesus would one day say, "In the world you will have tribulation" (John 16:33). However, what was His shout of victory over suffering (see John 16:33 again)?

(P.S. Looking ahead to John 19:25, to what was Simeon referring in Luke 2:35?)

Flight by Faith

Read Matthew 2:16 and briefly describe something else that happened next after Jesus' arrival.

How did God act to save the baby Jesus and His parents (Matthew 2:13-15)?

And how did God guide them back (verses 19-23)?

Thought: Aren't you glad Mary listened to Joseph and followed her husband's leading?

Joys and Sorrows

I know our lesson is getting a little long, but isn't it an exciting one! Wow, when you think of what Mary experienced (and at such a young age!), you better understand why she was so remarkable!

Now check the list of the *joys* and the *sorrows* Mary experienced. Do you agree or disagree that "motherhood is a painful privilege"?

And yet, what is a mother called to do according to Titus 2:4?

Aren't you glad God's grace is always sufficient!

Mary's Message
for Your Life Today

Please read this section in your book again. As you
consider the contents of this chapter and the pressures
or demands of your life, what main message spoke to
your heart…and how can you use that message to better
your life today?

_____

_____

_____

_____

_____

_____

_____

_____

_____

_____

_____

Remarkable Life

A Portrait of Devotion

Mary *"kept all these things in her heart."*
LUKE 2:51

~

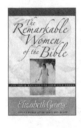

In your copy of *The Remarkable Women of the Bible,* read the chapter that is titled "A Portrait of Devotion." Make notes here about what meant the most to you from this chapter, offered you the greatest challenge, or helped you grow as a woman.

Sacred Devotion

A practical way Mary and Joseph lived out their devotion to God involved formal worship and family worship. Read now in Luke 2:41-50 about the details of one of their annual pilgrimages to Jerusalem. What was the occasion for the trip (verse 41)?

And what made this trip even more special (verse 42)?

"Mary, Did You Know?"

"Mary, Did You Know?" is a song (by Mark Lowry and Buddy Greene) that seems to express what happened there in Jerusalem. Look again at the description of that remarkable time in Luke 2:41-50. All was well. The Feast was over, and the elated groups began their trek home.

> What happened in verses 43-44 that caused concern in Mary and Joseph's hearts?

> Once Jesus' parents realized He was nowhere to be found in the group, what did they do (verse 45)?

> How long did their search take...and where did they finally find Jesus (verse 46)?

> What was the Boy Jesus doing there (verse 46)?

> And what was the response of the people...and why (verse 47)?

> Out of her heart poured forth Mary's anxiety! What did she want to know of Jesus (verse 48)?

> And what did Jesus want to know of Mary (verse 49)? (And remember, these are the first recorded words of Jesus in the Bible!)

And the result (verse 50)?

A High Calling

No, dear one, Mary would never understand! And neither will anyone, including you and me. Why? Because the appearance of Jesus, God "manifested in the flesh," is considered to be "the *mystery* of godliness" (1 Timothy 3:16). However, God allowed Mary to contribute to Jesus' life on earth, to have a role in His life. Note these high callings and take time to apply them to your contribution to your own dear family— your role of service to your loved ones.

Mary gave Jesus life—

Mary gave Jesus a home—

Mary gave Jesus a model of godliness—

Now, how can you better follow in Mary's faithful footsteps? What changes need to occur or what behaviors need to be corrected?

Devoted to the End

Revisit the mysterious and "piercing" words of Simeon in Luke 2:35. What did he say to Mary on that day in the Temple?

How, according to John 19:25, did Simeon's prophecy come true and when and where?

Oh, the pain! As we noted earlier, motherhood carries with it the dual emotions of joy *and* sorrow! Yet Mary was devoted to her Son to the end, regardless of the gruesomeness or the risk. And, beloved, her Son Jesus was devoted to the end to His dear suffering mother! What happened in John 19:26-27?

Be sure to copy out the two lessons Mary—and Jesus!—teach us regarding pain...and devotion to the end in spite of pain.

Lesson #1—

Lesson #2—

A Portrait of Devotion

I love the Bible's last glimpse of the remarkable life of Mary. (Or should I say, the remarkable life of the *humble* Mary?) See it for yourself in Acts 1:1-14.

According to verses 3-4, what happened?

What promise did the risen Christ give to His faithful followers (verse 5)?

And what instructions did He give them in verses 6-8?

And how did this scene end (verses 9-11)?

What did the band of faithful followers do next, according to verses 13-14?

And where do we find Mary and what is she doing (verse 14)?

Thus ends the remarkable life of Mary. She is never mentioned or referred to again in the Bible. What a wonderful memory of the woman who "found favor with God" (Luke 1:30)! Record now from your book the details of Mary's portrait of devotion as seen in her final appearance.

Fact #1—

Fact #2—

Fact #3—

Fact #4—

Fact #5—

Mary's Message
for Your Life Today

Please read this section in your book again. As you consider the contents of this chapter and the pressures or demands of your life, what main message spoke to your heart...and how can you use that message to better your life today?

_____

_____

_____

_____

_____

_____

_____

_____

_____

_____

Chapter 23

Two Faces of Love

"And [Martha] had a sister called Mary."
Luke 10:39

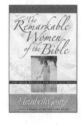 In your copy of *The Remarkable Women of the Bible,* read the chapter that is titled "Two Faces of Love." Make notes here about what meant the most to you from this chapter, offered you the greatest challenge, or helped you grow as a woman.

Peace or Panic?

Every married woman has heard these words, "Honey, guess who's coming to dinner?" And it always seems that the more important the dinner guest, the more the panic level rises! Well, that's what happened to two sisters. Read their story in Luke 10:38-42 and observe how this twosome reacted and responded to the most important dinner guest of all time—Jesus Christ.

To begin, who was waiting at the door when Jesus arrived (verse 38)?

What was her sister's name, and what was her sister's response to Jesus' presence (verse 39)?

And how did Martha respond to Jesus' presence (verse 40)?

What was Jesus' comment on Martha's response (verse 41)?

And what was Jesus' commendation concerning Mary's attitude (verse 42)?

With which sister do you normally identify when things get hectic and seem to be out of your control? And why?

How can Psalm 31:15 help you when panic starts to take over your peace?

And Isaiah 26:3?

And Philippians 4:13?

The Ultimate Resource

Now read John 11:1-3 and describe Mary and Martha's reactions to their brother's sickness.

What is your normal first response when a crisis occurs, and how do Mary and Martha show you a good–better–best way?

How might these verses help you to respond in a more biblical manner the next time there is a crisis (and believe me, there will be, so note them well!)?

Philippians 4:6-7—

Philippians 4:19—

2 Peter 1:3—

A Lesson in Faith

Describe Martha's actions at the arrival of Jesus in John 11:20.

What was Martha's reasoning in verse 21?

What was Martha's remorseful statement in verse 22?

At this point, what did Jesus state about Himself in verses 23-26?

What was Martha's realization in verse 27?

And you, dear friend? Having noted the things Jesus said about Himself, how would you answer Jesus' question to Martha, "Do you believe this?" And why?

Fruit Grown in the Shade

Now describe Mary's actions at the arrival of Jesus in John 11:20.

Read John 11:28-32 and compare the responses of the two sisters. What was similar and what was different?

How similar was Mary's posture in Luke 10:39 to this encounter with Jesus?

How would you describe your attitude of worship? In other words are you a Martha or a Mary? And why?

What good points or "messages" can you take away from each sister?

Two Faces of Love

We again meet up with Mary and Martha in John 12:1-8. And we again see how each of these remarkable sisters demonstrated her love for Jesus. Read about the scene now.

How (as usual!) did Martha show her love for Jesus?

And how did Mary show her love?

Now do you understand why I entitled this chapter and lesson "Two Faces of Love"? Martha's love was demonstrated by her _____, and Mary's love was demonstrated by her _____.

Bonus question: What was the response of at least one of Jesus' disciples to Mary's sacrificial act of worship (verses 4-5)? Or, put another way, how was Mary's worship misunderstood? Or, put still another way, how was Mary ridiculed for her worship of Christ?

Now the question is, How can you balance your love for the Savior as you...

...serve?

...worship?

Mary and Martha's Message
for Your Life Today

Please read this section in your book again. As you consider the contents of this chapter and the pressures or demands of your life, what main message spoke to your heart...and how can you use that message to better your life today?

_____

_____

_____

_____

_____

_____

_____

_____

_____

_____

Selfless Service

She has "diligently followed every good work."
1 TIMOTHY 5:10

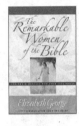 In your copy of *The Remarkable Women of the Bible*, read the chapter that is titled "Selfless Service." Make notes here about what meant the most to you from this chapter, offered you the greatest challenge, or helped you grow as a woman.

Dorcas—The Eyes of Love

In this lesson we have the honor and privilege of looking at four remarkable servants in the New Testament church. Begin by reading Dorcas' story in Acts 9:36-43.

> Write out the "service record" of this dear saint-of-old recorded in Acts 9:36.

What was a tangible product of Dorcas' ministry in her local church (see Acts 9:39)?

Now for you (and me and every Christian woman!)—What could be written about your service record? Write out a one-sentence description of your service to the people in your church. If you can't think of anything, what can you do today to develop eyes of love? (P.S. How does 1 Peter 4:8 help? And also verses 9-11?)

Lydia—The Power of a Woman

Lydia was a remarkable woman who was quite unique in her day. Very few women are mentioned in the New Testament who had what we call today a profession and a business. Lydia was a modern-day phenomenon—a career woman! In our time, it is estimated that 50 percent of married women work at a job outside the home. So Lydia's message is relevant for both single and married women alike.

Read Lydia's story now in Acts 16:11-15,40.

Where do we first meet this woman, and why was she there (verse 13)?

How did God work in her heart, and through whom (verse 14)?

What was Lydia's first act of obedience as a Christian, as a believer in Jesus Christ (verse 15)?

And what was her first act of service (verse 15)?

As time passed, Lydia continued to serve the Lord and His people. What ministry is she providing the church in verse 40?

Lydia was a worshiper who was spiritually attentive and who was baptized. She was hospitable, generous, and a woman of great power and influence in the early church. How do you measure up to Lydia's example? How do you measure up as a servant of the Lord and of His people? Pick one of Lydia's powerful qualities, devise a plan for maturing in this area, and put your plan into action this week. Now, what is the quality, and what is your plan?

Lydia—The Purpose of Wealth

We've already noted that Lydia was a businesswoman. What exactly was her business (Acts 16:14)?

As a businesswoman, Lydia possessed some wealth. But as a Christian, Lydia understood the purpose of wealth. She understood that her wealth was to be shared for the good of others. Therefore she was generous and hospitable. What is the exhortation for the use of our money in 1 Timothy 6:18?

Now what do you have (wealth or otherwise) that you can share with others?

Priscilla—Bookends

Priscilla and her husband, Aquila, provide a great model of a couple who was sold out in service to their Lord. Note their mutual ministry in these instances:

Acts 18:1-3—

Acts 18:18-19—

Acts 18:24-26—

1 Corinthians 16:19—

2 Timothy 4:19—

I know many Christian women who are in a marriage situation where they must shoulder all or most of the spiritual responsibility for the home (and you may be just such a woman). But regardless of your situation, you can still follow in Sister Priscilla's footsteps. In your own words, what do you see Priscilla doing that you can do?

Priscilla—Suffering and Glory

Sounds exciting, doesn't it? Go anywhere at any time...to serve God? Rubbing shoulders with the greats...such as the apostle Paul and the eloquent Apollos? But all was not bliss for Priscilla and her husband (nor is it for anyone who serves the Lord!). What do we learn about this dynamic duo in Romans 16:3-4?

Expect suffering!
What does Paul say about the one who lives a godly life in 2 Timothy 3:12?

Rejoice in suffering!
And what does the apostle Peter say about suffering in 1 Peter 4:12-13?

How do Priscilla, Aquila, Paul, and Peter change your thoughts about suffering as you serve Christ?

Phoebe—A Shining Servant

Service and faithfulness go hand in hand, don't they? If you're not sure, look at Romans 16:1-2. This is where we hear about the remarkable service of Phoebe. How does the apostle Paul describe her? *(Warning:* Don't go too quickly! Paul packed a lot into these two verses! Phoebe was quite a lady!)

Just think (humanly speaking, that is), what if Phoebe had just not gotten "around to it" when it came to taking that letter (the book of Romans!) with her to Rome. Or what if she had carelessly lost or misplaced it? Are you getting the picture when it comes to the importance of faithfulness? I know it's something I work on every day of my life! How do you rate yourself on the Faithfulness Scale, and what can you do to improve?

And by the way, what is one quality Paul says proves a woman's maturity for service in the church in 1 Timothy 3:11?

Phoebe—Selfless Service

Bonus question: How do Phoebe's humble acts of service (indeed, those of all four of these remarkable servants!) inspire you to be more faithful in service to your family, your church, and other people?

Dorcas, Lydia, Priscilla, and Phoebe's Message for Your Life Today

Please read this section in your book again. As you consider the contents of this chapter and the pressures or demands of your life, what main message spoke to your heart...and how can you use that message to better your life today?

_____

_____

_____

_____

_____

_____

_____

_____

_____

_____

A Final Look

"Now faith is the substance of things hoped for,
the evidence of things not seen."
HEBREWS 11:1

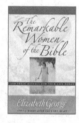 In your copy of *The Remarkable Women of the Bible,* read the summary that is titled "Queens of Remarkable Faith and Grace." Make notes here about what meant the most to you from this conclusion, offered you the greatest challenge, or helped you grow as a woman.

As we say farewell to these dear women of remarkable faith and grace, we want to take their messages along with us. We don't want to be guilty of wasting the time we've spent *discovering* God's messages to our hearts from these women's remarkable lives by not creating some kind of record for *remembering* them for prayer, for application, and for change. After all, what is the Bible but God's Word! And what is its purpose according to 2 Timothy 3:16-17?

We also don't want to be guilty of the behavior of the man pictured in James 1:23-24. What did he do?

What is our goal instead, as seen in James 1:22?

And as seen in 2 Peter 3:18?

So, in order to be doers of the Word, and not merely hearers (or readers!), and in order to grow in grace and knowledge ourselves, let's do one more exercise. Recall—and record—God's most striking message to your heart from each remarkable life of the women in the Bible we met along the way through our book. And once again, dear faithful friend, ask God to help you write these timeless messages on the tablet of your heart (Proverbs 3:3)! May He richly bless you as you do so.

Queens of Remarkable Faith and Grace

Eve—

Sarah—

Rebekah—

Jochebed—

Miriam—

Rahab—

Deborah—

Queens of Remarkable Faith and Grace

Ruth and Naomi—

Hannah—

Esther—

Elizabeth—

Mary—

Mary and Martha—

Dorcas, Lydia, Priscilla, and Phoebe—

Leading a Bible Study Discussion Group

~

*W*hat a privilege it is to lead a Bible study! And what joy and excitement await you as you delve into the Word of God and help others to discover its life-changing truths. If God has called you to lead a Bible study group, I know you'll be spending much time in prayer and planning and giving much thought to being an effective leader. I also know that taking the time to read through the following tips will help you to navigate the challenges of leading a Bible study discussion group and enjoying the effort and opportunity.

The Leader's Roles

As a Bible study group leader, you'll find your role changing back and forth from *expert* to *cheerleader* to *lover* to *referee* during the course of a session.

Since you're the leader, group members will look to you to be the *expert* guiding them through the material. So be well prepared. In fact, be over-prepared so that you know the material better than any group member does. Start your study early in the week and let its message simmer all week long. (You might even work several lessons ahead so that you have in mind the big picture and the overall direction of the study.) Be ready to share some additional gems that your group members wouldn't have discovered on their own. That extra insight from your study time—or that comment from a wise Bible teacher or scholar, that clever saying, that keen observation from another believer, and even an appropriate joke—adds an element of fun and keeps Bible study from becoming routine, monotonous, and dry.

Next, be ready to be the group's *cheerleader*. Your energy and enthusiasm for the task at hand can be contagious. It can also stimulate people to get more involved in their personal study as well as in the group discussion.

Third, be the *lover*, the one who shows a genuine concern for the members of the group. You're the one who will establish the atmosphere of the group. If you laugh and have fun, the group members will laugh and have fun. If you hug, they will hug. If you care, they will care. If you share, they will share. If you love, they will love. So pray every day to love the women God has placed in your group. Ask Him to show you how to love them with His love.

Finally, as the leader, you'll need to be the *referee* on occasion. That means making sure everyone has an equal opportunity to speak. That's easier to do when you operate under the assumption that every member of the group has something worthwhile to contribute. So, trusting that the Lord has taught each person during the week, act on that assumption.

Expert, cheerleader, lover, and referee—these four roles of the leader may make the task seem overwhelming. But that's not bad if it keeps you on your knees praying for your group.

A Good Start

Beginning on time, greeting people warmly, and opening in prayer gets the study off to a good start. Know what you want to have happen during your time together and make sure those things get done. That kind of order means comfort for those involved.

Establish a format and let the group members know what that format is. People appreciate being in a Bible study that focuses on the Bible. So keep the discussion on the topic and move the group through the questions. Tangents are often hard to avoid—and even harder to rein in. So be sure to focus on the answers to questions about the specific passage at hand. After all, the purpose of the group is Bible study!

Finally, as someone has accurately observed, "Personal growth is one of the by-products of any effective small group. This growth is achieved when people are recognized and accepted by others. The more friendliness, mutual trust, respect, and warmth exhibited, the more likely that the member will find pleasure in the group, and, too, the more likely she will work hard toward the accomplishment of the group's goals. The effective leader will strive to reinforce desirable traits" (source unknown).

A Dozen Helpful Tips

Here is a list of helpful suggestions for leading a Bible study discussion group:

1. Arrive early, ready to focus fully on others and give of yourself. If you have to do any last-minute preparation, review, re-grouping, or praying, do it in the car. Don't dash in, breathless, harried, late, still tweaking your plans.

2. Check out your meeting place in advance. Do you have everything you need—tables, enough chairs, a blackboard, hymnals if you plan to sing, coffee, etc.?

3. Greet each person warmly by name as she arrives. After all, you've been praying for these women all week long, so let each VIP know that you're glad she's arrived.

4. Use name tags for at least the first two or three weeks.

5. Start on time no matter what—even if only one person is there!

6. Develop a pleasant but firm opening statement. You might say, "This lesson was great! Let's get started so we can enjoy all of it!" or "Let's pray before we begin our lesson."

7. Read the questions, but don't hesitate to reword them on occasion. Rather than reading an entire paragraph of instructions, for instance, you might say, "Question 1 asks us to list some ways that Christ displayed humility. Lisa, please share one way Christ displayed humility."

8. Summarize or paraphrase the answers given. Doing so will keep the discussion focused on the topic, eliminate digressions, help avoid or clear up any misunderstandings of the text, and keep each group member aware of what the others are saying.

9. Keep moving and don't add any of your own questions to the discussion time. It's important to get through the study guide questions. So if a cut-and-dried answer is called for, you don't need to comment with anything other than a "thank you." But when the question asks for an opinion or an application (for instance, "How can this truth help us in our marriages?" or "How do *you* find time for your quiet time?"), let all who want to contribute do so.

10. Affirm each person who contributes, especially if the contribution was very personal, painful to share, or a quiet person's rare statement. Make everyone who shares a hero by saying something like "Thank you for sharing that insight from your own life," or "We certainly appreciate what God has taught you. Thank you for letting us in on it."

11. Watch your watch, put a clock right in front of you, or consider using a timer. Pace the discussion so that you meet your cut-off time, especially if you want time to pray. Stop at the designated time even if you haven't finished the lesson. Remember that everyone has worked through the study once; you are simply going over it again.

12. End on time. You can only make friends with your group members by ending on time or even a little early! Besides, members of your group have the next item on their agenda to attend to—picking up children from the nursery, babysitter, or school; heading home to tend to matters there; running errands; getting to bed; or spending some time with their husbands. So let them out *on time!*

Five Common Problems

In any group, you can anticipate certain problems. Here are some common ones that can arise, along with helpful solutions:

1. *The incomplete lesson*—Right from the start, establish the policy that if someone has not done the lesson, it is best for her not to answer the questions. But do try to include her responses to questions that ask for opinions or experiences. Everyone can share some thoughts in reply to a question like, "Reflect on what you know about both

athletic and spiritual training and then share what you consider to be the essential elements of training oneself in godliness."

2. *The gossip*—The Bible clearly states that gossiping is wrong, so you don't want to allow it in your group. Set a high and strict standard by saying, "I am not comfortable with this conversation," or "We [not *you*] are gossiping, ladies. Let's move on."

3. *The talkative member*—Here are three scenarios and some possible solutions for each.

   a. The problem talker may be talking because she has done her homework and is excited about something she has to share. She may also know more about the subject than the others and, if you cut her off, the rest of the group may suffer.

   SOLUTION: Respond with a comment like: "Sarah, you are making very valuable contributions. Let's see if we can get some reactions from the others," or "I know Sarah can answer this. She's really done her homework. How about some of the rest of you?"

   b. The talkative member may be talking because she has *not* done her homework and wants to contribute, but she has no boundaries.

   SOLUTION: Establish at the first meeting that those who have not done the lesson do not contribute except on opinion or application questions. You may need to repeat this guideline at the beginning of each session.

   c. The talkative member may want to be heard whether or not she has anything worthwhile to contribute.

SOLUTION: After subtle reminders, be more direct, saying, "Betty, I know you would like to share your ideas, but let's give others a chance. I'll call on you later."

4. *The quiet member*—Here are two scenarios and possible solutions.

   a. The quiet member wants the floor but somehow can't get the chance to share.

   SOLUTION: Clear the path for the quiet member by first watching for clues that she wants to speak (moving to the edge of her seat, looking as if she wants to speak, perhaps even starting to say something) and then saying, "Just a second. I think Chris wants to say something." Then, of course, make her a hero!

   b. The quiet member simply doesn't want the floor.

   SOLUTION: "Chris, what answer do you have on question 2?" or "Chris, what do you think about...?" Usually after a shy person has contributed a few times, she will become more confident and more ready to share. Your role is to provide an opportunity where there is *no* risk of a wrong answer. But occasionally a group member will tell you that she would rather not be called on. Honor her request, but from time to time ask her privately if she feels ready to contribute to the group discussions.

   In fact, give all your group members the right to pass. During your first meeting, explain that any time a group member does not care to share an answer, she may simply say, "I pass." You'll want to repeat this policy at the beginning of every group session.

5. *The wrong answer*—Never tell a group member that she has given a wrong answer, but at the same time never let a wrong answer go by.

>   **SOLUTION:** Either ask if someone else has a different answer or ask additional questions that will cause the right answer to emerge. As the women get closer to the right answer, say, "We're getting warmer! Keep thinking! We're almost there!"

Learning from Experience

Immediately after each Bible study session, evaluate the group discussion time using this checklist. You may also want a member of your group (or an assistant or trainee or outside observer) to evaluate you periodically.

May God strengthen—and encourage!—you as you assist others in the discovery of His many wonderful truths.

A Woman After God's Own Heart® Study Series

BIBLE STUDIES FOR BUSY WOMEN

"God wrote the Bible to change hearts and lives. Every study in this series is written with that in mind—and is specially focused on helping Christian women know how God desires for them to live."

—Elizabeth George

Sharing wisdom gleaned from more than 20 years as a women's Bible study teacher, Elizabeth has prepared insightful lessons that can be completed in 15 to 20 minutes per day. Each lesson includes thought-provoking questions and insights, Bible study tips, instructions for leading a discussion group, and a "heart response" section to make the Bible passage more personal.

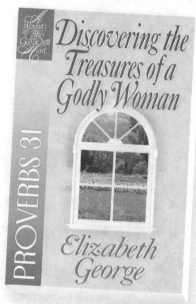

Proverbs 31 0-7369-0818-8

Philippians 0-7369-0289-9

1 Peter 0-7369-0290-2

1 Timothy 0-7369-0665-7

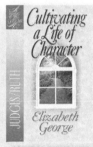

Judges/Ruth 0-7369-0498-0

Esther 0-7369-0489-1

James 0-7369-0490-5

Life of Mary 0-7369-0300-3

Life of Sarah 0-7369-0301-1

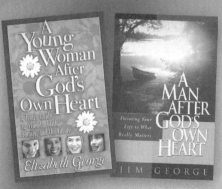
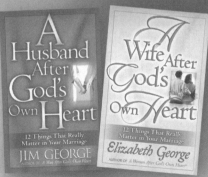

Books by Elizabeth George

Beautiful in God's Eyes—The Treasures of the Proverbs 31 Woman
God's Wisdom for Every Woman's Life
Life Management for Busy Women
Loving God with All Your Mind
Powerful Promises™ for Every Couple
Powerful Promises™ for Every Woman
The Remarkable Women of the Bible
A Wife After God's Own Heart
A Woman After God's Own Heart®
A Woman After God's Own Heart® Deluxe Edition
A Woman After God's Own Heart® Prayer Journal
A Woman's Call to Prayer
A Woman's High Calling
A Woman's Walk with God
A Young Woman After God's Own Heart

Growth & Study Guides

God's Wisdom for Every Woman's Life Growth & Study Guide
Life Management for Busy Women Growth & Study Guide
Powerful Promises™ for Every Couple Growth & Study Guide
Powerful Promises™ for Every Woman Growth & Study Guide
The Remarkable Women of the Bible Growth & Study Guide
A Wife After God's Own Heart Growth & Study Guide
A Woman's Call to Prayer Growth & Study Guide
A Woman After God's Own Heart® Growth & Study Guide
A Woman's High Calling Growth & Study Guide
A Woman's Walk with God Growth & Study Guide

A Woman After God's Own Heart® Bible Study Series

Walking in God's Promises—The Life of Sarah
Cultivating a Life of Character—Judges/Ruth
Becoming a Woman of Beauty & Strength—Esther
Discovering the Treasures of a Godly Woman—Proverbs 31
Nurturing a Heart of Humility—The Life of Mary
Experiencing God's Peace—Philippians
Pursuing Godliness—1 Timothy
Growing in Wisdom & Faith—James
Putting On a Gentle & Quiet Spirit—1 Peter

Children's Books

God Loves His Precious Children
God's Wisdom for Little Boys—Character-Building Fun from Proverbs
(co-authored with Jim George)
God's Wisdom for Little Girls—Virtues & Fun from Proverbs 31